Trade Secrets of a Haircolor Expert

Presents

Exotic Brunettes

David Velasco

Disclaimer

This course is designed to educate and inform its readers of the subject matter covered herein. The publisher and author do not warrant any guarantee or responsibility to any person or entity with respect to any loss or damage caused directly or indirectly by the information contained in this book. The reader is expressly warned to consider and adopt all safety precautions that might be indicated by the activities herein and to avoid all potential hazards. By following the instructions contained herein, the reader willingly assumes all risk and liability in connection with such instructions.

WHAT INDUSTRY LEADERS ARE SAYING ABOUT "TRADE SECRETS"

In the early 1990s, I made this decision to switch to Wella Hair exclusively for the Bumble and bumble salon. As we had been using a mixture of 4/5 hair color brands, this was an extremely difficult transition. At that time, we had nine colorists and we were one of the busiest salons in New York. The first week of transition was extremely difficult with everyone completely confused and the results were varied.

It was at this point that I first met David Velasco. He had just finished a long stint as the art director and head colorist for Wella US and he very much wanted to come work at Bumble. I hired him specifically to try and help us make sense of this new color methodology that we were going to be using. With David's help, things changed and improved almost immediately. Apart from his quiet leadership and charismatic way, he was simply never ruffled. Further, he has a very deep understanding of the basic concepts of hair color as well as the complex tasks that some clients choose to do. He managed very quickly to make sure that all nine colorists were confident in the new haircolor and made sure they continued to broaden the skills and knowledge that they were missing and strengthen their techniques. His overall personality and experience were huge boosts to a salon that had over 120 employees.

After five years, David decided to return to his own salon. However, he had made an indelible mark on the quality of work that our hair color department was able to produce. I would say that every salon in America should have this book series. It is a must read, must know, must study book.

Michael A. Gordon
Founder
Bumble and bumble

David,

When you told me that you were writing a book I knew that it would be good,
but what you wrote is the encyclopedia of haircolor!

Dee Levin
Salon Nornandee
Secretary of Intercoiffure-America

Dear David,

I was reading your book again tonight. I must say, you have some INCREDIBLE CONTENT! You have a FABULOUS OPPORTUNITY to set a higher tone for haircolor education.

I think this book could set a new standard for "Non-manufacturer" education. You have done an EXQUISITE job writing a truly definitive work.
Again, your content is PHENOMENAL!
Wishing you all the very best! Stay in touch, -- you are on to something very special. This shows what a wonderful teacher you are.

Beth!

Beth Minardi

David,

I have just finished the first four chapters of your book and I must tell you that it is one of the best haircolor books I have ever seen.

One of the easiest to follow, great comments on the 'trade secrets', non commercial, and it is very obvious that you have a lot of knowledge and experience on haircolor from being behind the chair.

I look forward to reading the rest of the book and to seeing you in September

Fondly,
Sheila

Sheila Zaricor
Treasurer - International Haircolor Exchange

What You Will Learn in this Book

Exotic Brunettes

Introduction

<u>*Knowledge is Power*</u>

Knowledge is power. This power is having confidence in your skills and abilities as a professional haircolorist: the power to create beauty and make people feel great about themselves; the power to distinguish yourself as an authority in your field and gain praise and recognition from your peers and community. And, of course, this power translates into increasing your income according to your expertise.

Yes, I know all of this can come true for you. How do I know? Because it happened to me and I have seen it happen to many hairdressers to whom I have had the pleasure of teaching these techniques and strategies over my thirty plus years in the beauty industry.

You hold in your hands the power to achieve all of this and more.

Napoleon Hill, famed author of one of the best personal achievement book ever written, *Think and Grow Rich,* called this type of knowledge "Specialized Knowledge" and it is #4 in his history-making book.

He goes on to say that Specialized Knowledge is the kind that inspired people like Henry Ford and Thomas Edison to go on and achieve greatness in their lifetimes. This type of greatness cannot be achieved with only general knowledge.

I am not saying that once you have studied this course, you will become the next Bill Gates of haircolor, but once you read and internalize the information in this course, it does have the power to change your career and your life forever.

Why This Course is Titled:
Trade Secrets of a Haircolor Expert

> ***Webster's Dictionary defines TRADE SECRET as:***
>
> Main Entry: **trade secret**
> Function: *noun*
> something (as a formula) which has economic value to a business because it is not generally known or easily discoverable by observation.

> ***The Wikipedia online encyclopedia defines TRADE SECRET as:***
>
> A **trade secret** is a formula, practice, process, design, or compilation of information used by a business to obtain an advantage over competitors.

In this course, you will learn many formulation concepts that are not generally known by the masses of hairdressers. Sure, some of them will seem familiar to you and you may have heard them somewhere along the line in your training. However, hearing something and learning how to use what you have heard are two very different things.

The main thing that is going to set you apart from your competition, giving you the status and recognition as a Haircolor Expert in your community is knowledge, not just any kind of knowledge, but, as stated before, "Specialized Knowledge".

You can only get this kind of knowledge two ways - by learning from trial and error (this will take years) or by learning from someone that has been there before you. Specialized Knowledge will not be found in the textbooks in our industry or by going to weekend hair shows that are designed to entertain hairdressers and sell products.

When I first started to learn haircolor, well known hair colorists at that time used to keep their formulations under lock and key. They literally had metal strong boxes that they kept their client color cards in so that no one could steal their formulas.

Thank God, today things are different. Most haircolorist are willing to share their ideas and color concepts with others. But the question now becomes - whose way is right; whose way is best and who's willing to guide me step-by-step through every haircolor procedure until I have the confidence to go it alone?

Exotic Brunettes

In this course, you will find the Trade Secrets that will give you the confidence to go it alone, and, as a side benefit, you will also shave many years off of your learning curve. Instead of taking years and learning by trial and error, you will be able to refer back to this information over and over again throughout your career.

How to Use This Course

This course is laid out in a progressive knowledge-based sequence.
The first two volumes, *Haircolor 101- The Beginning* and *How Haircolor Really Works*, are "must read" books. The information in these two books must be understood before moving on to the other books. In these books, you will learn the theories, techniques and strategies that I will refer to over and over as you progress through the rest of the course.

Also, if you are experiencing gray coverage problems, I highly recommend reading Volume 3, *Great Gray Coverage* next. In this book you will learn 9 strategies for covering gray hair as well as how to work with gray hair in every conceivable situation.

After you have studied these three books, feel free to jump around to the other books as you wish.

In each of the other books, you will find an introduction to that particular segment of the course, followed by special formulation strategies that will guarantee you success in performing every possible haircolor situation. Towards the end of each chapter, is a color correction section that will guide you, step-by-step through any haircolor problem that you will ever encounter.

Exotic Brunettes

In this color correction section, you will not only learn **how** to fix every haircolor problem you will ever encounter, but you will also learn **why** this problem occurred and **how to prevent** it from happening in the future.

Also, so that colorists around the world can utilize this course, no specific product name or shade is mentioned. Instead, in each haircolor situation in this course, every effort has been made to refer to the formulation by **level & tone** only. Therefore, it doesn't matter what haircolor manufacturer or brand name you are using, you will still be able to utilize all the information in this course.

Once you have internalized this information, you will see your creativity expand, feel your confidence grow and be well on your way to becoming a haircolor specialist and a true expert in the field.

I truly wish you much success in your journey of becoming a haircolor expert and I would love to hear from you about your success along the way. Also, if you happen to encounter a haircolor situation that you cannot find the answer to in this course, please don't hesitate to email me at david@dvsalon.com and I will gladly assist you in any way I can.

I wish you massive success in all your haircolor endeavors,

David Velasco

PS: As a thank you for purchesing this book, I would like to give you a **FREE 128 Page Haircolor E-Book, 7 Steps to Haircolor Mastery. T**o download it, go to:

www.HaircolorTradeSecrets.com

EXOTIC BRUNETTES

Introduction

Exotic, Romantic and Seductive are words used to describe brunettes. In the United States blonde hair and blue eyes are usually used to describe the all-American look. However, brunettes throughout the ages have always had a special place in our hearts.

Elizabeth Taylor, Liz Hurley and Angelina Jolie are great examples of brunettes that come to mind as exotic, romantic and seductive. Also some of the most famous "blondes" in the past century were in fact brunettes: Jean Harlow, Marilyn Monroe, and Bridget Bardot. As a matter of fact, I personally like brunettes so much that I married one.

At first, one may think that making someone a brunette is a simple task for a colorist to do. But the truth is that making a good, rich brunette can be very challenging. Again, as in every haircolor situation, porosity plays a major role in the making of a great brunette.

If the hair is overly porous, a dark brown brunette will easily become black. Trying to make a brunette slightly lighter may result in an unwanted red shade. Uneven porosity could result in dark temples, dark ends and a reddish root area. I am not saying this to scare you, but if you've ever had one of these situations and didn't know what happened or how to correct this mistake, you know what I am talking about.

Exotic Brunettes

Let's start our discussion about brunettes by establishing what a brunette is. To me, a brunette can be anyone with a level 1 to 5 (black to light brown) that has a rich brown tone. Brunettes can be warm (gold or red-brown base) or cool (ash or neutral / natural base).

NOTE: Reddish brown is discussed here as a brunette color because when natural brown is lightened, it will always produce a warm color in the reddish brown family. This does not mean that all darker reds such as auburn or burgundy should be considered brunettes. In my opinion, these are redheads and are discussed in the "Amazing Redheads" book.

Exotic Brunettes

The Best Candidates for
Warm and Cool Brunettes

Levels 1-5

Any natural level (1-10) can become a tinted brunette shade, but, keep in mind, darker natural levels (levels 1-5) will have a strong red-orange exposed contributing pigment when a tint is applied.

It is for this reason that I really prefer to use a demi type color, if possible. It will create less warmth (because they produce less lift) than a permanent color in the same level.

This red-orange contributing pigment makes it almost impossible to create a cool natural looking brunette unless you go very dark (which may not look very natural).

Levels 6-10

Making a cool brunette out of someone in levels 6-10 will be quite easy to do because you won't be fighting the unwanted warm pigment.

Making a warm brown out of levels 6-10 is not a difficult task because color manufacturers have given us many wonderful warm gold and red shades that will produce very adequate results even on 100% Gray (non-pigmented) hair.

The chart on the next page shows the exposed contributing pigment you can expect to see in the hair as the tint begins to fade.

The main thing to remember is:

Haircolor Secret
Less Lift = Less Warmth

THE BEST CANDIDATES FOR WARM AND COOL BRUNETTES

NATURAL HAIRCOLOR	LEVEL	CONTRIBUTING COLOR PIGMENT	
LIGHTEST BLONDE	10	PALE YELLOW →	
VERY LIGHT BLONDE	9	YELLOW →	LEVELS – 6 to 10 Best for Cool Brunettes
LIGHT BLONDE	8	DARK YELLOW →	
MEDIUM BLONDE	7	GOLD →	
DARK BLONDE	6	GOLD ORANGE →	
LIGHT BROWN	5	ORANGE →	
MEDIUM BROWN	4	RED ORANGE →	LEVELS – 1 to 5 Best for Warm Brunettes
DARK BROWN	3	DARK RED ORANGE →	
VERY DARK	2	RED BROWN →	
BLACK	1	DARK RED BROWN →	

2 Ground Rules for Brunettes

Now, we need to establish a couple ground rules about tinting someone's hair brown.

Ground Rule #1

Haircolor Secret
Any time you apply an oxidative tint to the hair, *you are going to get some warmth.*

Because all tint works on the premise that it must lift (lighten) the natural haircolor to some degree before it can tint the hair to the desired shade, we must always be aware of how much lift we are asking the tint to do.

It is here that we must learn to control the lifting action or we will expose too much of the hair's contributing color pigment, thus producing too much warmth (reddish tone) and causing premature fading.

Ground Rule #2

Haircolor Secret

If you are going to use an ash base color in order to control the unwanted warm tone, keep in mind that ash colors don't always work as well as we wish they would.

Many times the dark blue or green pigment in these colors will cause the tint to go too dark. Then again, if your tone isn't dark enough, you will still get unwanted warm tones. Maybe not the day that the service is done, but within a few weeks, it will become warm.

In this book I'll give you several techniques to use for creating great looking rich brunettes and correct whatever problems you may experience with your brunette clients.

Keeping a Natural Brunette, Brunette

As brunette baby boomers begin to age, a few changes start to occur in their hair. First, the deep rich tone that they once had as a youngster or young adult will begin to fade and lack the luster that they once had. Then, as the hair begins to turn gray, many times, it will take on a very flat, lifeless look or turn a strange reddish color as the natural course of de-pigmentation starts taking place.

Once brunette hair turns gray, it seems to stick out like a sore thumb against the backdrop of the darker pigmented hair. So what can be done about this undesirable situation?

My recommendation is to use a demi-color on these clients, if the goal is to regain the natural color and luster that these clients have lost and to color the gray at the same time.

I would only use a permanent haircolor if I absolutely could not get a demi-color to cover the gray adequately. This is because, if you use a permanent haircolor on a natural brunette that has some gray, all of the rest of the hair (still dark pigmented) will be subjected to the full impact of the ammonia and peroxide. In a few short weeks, as the tint begins to fade (as all tints will), her once brown hair will become a reddish brown.

However, given this same scenario, if using a demi-color, you will be creating much less lift (if any) due to the less aggressive effect that demi-colors have on the hair.

Even though demi-colors are mixed with some kind of catalyst (ammonia, peroxide or sometimes both), it still is in such small quantities when compared to permanent haircolor (even level 1 black). It is definitely worth a try before you resort to permanent haircolor.

Making Salt & Pepper Hair Rich Brown

Again, I would use the demi-colors first and try to do the job without exposing unnecessary contributing reddish natural color pigment. In this case, I would formulate to match the pepper (darker hair) and not try to lighten up the dark at all. Remember, lifting the natural color will bring a warm (reddish) result.

If you are having trouble getting the demi-color to give you good gray coverage, read the book, *Trade Secrets of Great Gray Coverage* in this course. In that book, you will learn many ways to tweak a demi-color to make it perform better for you.

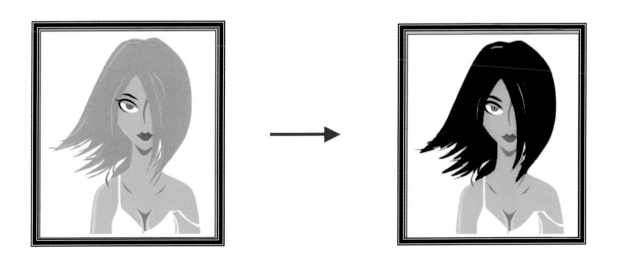

Making 75-100% Gray (non-pigmented)
Hair Brunette

Once again, my first choice would be to try a demi-color and utilize a few of my gray coverage secrets, which I discussed in the book, ***Trade Secrets of Great Gray Coverage,*** before I would reach for my so-called "permanent" haircolor. There is a reason for this. Let me explain…

A permanent hair color would definitely give me very good gray coverage. But as I've already said, as the color fades, the hair will become very warm, even on gray (non-pigmented)/White hair. Remember, non-pigmented/white hair still has Pheomelanin (red-yellow) pigment in it. Also, as far as coverage is concerned, many times a dark level permanent haircolor could look too opaque (solid dark color) and, therefore, very artificial - like shoe polish.

Once again, I feel that demi-colors tend to produce much more natural looking haircolor results due to the fact that the direct dyes will deposit pigmentation equally over the entire head of unequal natural haircolor. Therefore, where the hair still has some darker strands it will get darker.

The non-pigmented/white hair will get dark, but not as dark as the tinted pigmented hair.

Haircolor Secret

Depth on top of depth will always produce more depth.

Depth on top of white produces a darker tone,

but not as dark as depth on top of depth.

The end product will have some gradation of tone and not a heavy, solid opaque look. As the demi-color begins to fade, remember that it will fade on tone, not off tone. Therefore, a deep rich brunette produced with a demi-color will become a lighter shade of brown, as it begins to fade. A deep, rich brunette produced with a permanent color will fade off tone into the red family. Which would your client prefer?

Making a Natural Blonde a Brunette

I am not sure why you would ever want to do this, given the fact that natural blondes are so beautiful on their own. However, if you ever need to do it, here's how it's done.

This will be a very easy and straightforward procedure, if the hair is in good condition. By nature, a natural blonde should have some warmth in her hair (gold). All you have to do is select the shade you want to use (demi or permanent) and simply apply the tint from re-growth to ends.

The only thing to be careful of is if the ends are dry or overly porous. If that is the case, use a light gold demi-color on the ends first as a filler for about 15 minutes or so, then apply your desired shade over the whole thing. Shampoo when the desired shade has been reached.

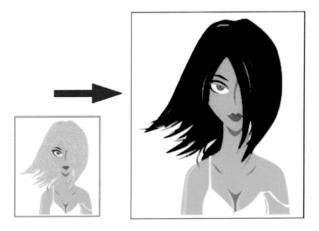

Making a Natural Redhead a Brunette

If you have a request for this, the first thing you want to do is have your client's head examined. But if she still wants to follow through with the procedure, then here's how.

Once again, if the hair is in good condition, simply mix your desired shade (demi or permanent) and apply re-growth to ends.

The only thing you need to be aware of is that natural red is the hardest of all hair colors to change. This is true if you are lightening or darkening. Because red pigment, by far, is the hardest to cover or remove from the hair, I am making the following recommendation to you.

You should go at least 2 levels darker than your client's natural hair color in order to cancel out the warm tone. Of course, you should use an ash base tint to help subdue the unwanted red tone. Make sure you do a strand test first so that you don't go too dark and have your client freak out.

Once again, I would try using a demi-color first. If you end up using a permanent color, you will be exposing your client's hair to even more of this already present (and unwanted) red color pigment.

Making a Double Process Blonde a Brunette

Now this can be very tricky, but, if you read this lesson carefully, you will not have any problems and create a truly beautiful brunette when you're done.

By the way, this procedure is not only used for converting a double process blonde into a brunette. You should also use this procedure any time you are converting any highly porous head of hair to a darker, warmer (brown or red) color.

The key factor isn't the method of how the hair becomes lighter, it is the absence of warmth (gold and red) in the hair and the condition of the hair that will be the determining factors for using this method or not.

NOTE: This procedure is commonly known as a tint-back and will also be discussed in other sections of this course.

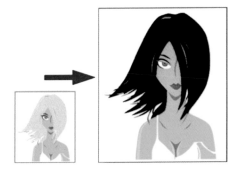

Tint Backs….

The Overall Concept: If you remember from your beauty school days, as you lighten out hair, it goes through what is called the "Stages of Lift". It goes something like this…

Brown→Reddish Brown→Red→Orange→ Gold→Yellow→Pale Yellow

Brown to Blonde

So if we want to make a brunette out of pale yellow hair, we would need to replace the colors which were lightened out in the same order as they were depleted. In order to make the job a lot easier, we can use an orange (yellow & red pre-mixed) demi-color instead of applying a gold then red color.

Blonde to Brown

Pale Yellow→Yellow→Gold→Orange→Red→Reddish Brown→Brown

Exotic Brunettes

You never want to use any ash tones in this procedure. Even if you want your finished color to look ashy, you must still use a gold or neutral base color as your final shade. Never use a green, blue, or violet shade tint.

Tint backs are when you are taking a client that has been getting her hair lightened out (as in a double process blonde or a very light single process blonde with a high degree of porosity), back to her natural color or to any darker color than she presently is.

In this case, we will use the exposed contributing pigment chart from the beginning of this book to see what colors need to be put back into the hair before you can achieve a natural looking finished result. (This technique is sometimes called **"Color Packing"** or replacing the **"Building Blocks of Color"**).

For example:

The client has been double processed for some time now and wishes to go back to her natural color, which was a "level 4, light brown". Remember, you cannot just select a light brown tint, put it on this bleached out hair and expect to get a good color. There isn't a sufficient color base left in the hair to support the light brown color. The hair will grab the base of the tint and come out looking very drab, muddy or green. You must first put the missing contributing pigment back into the hair before applying the final desired shade.

You can see by looking at the chart on the next page, that, in order to make a "level 4, light brown", the missing contributing pigment must be put back into the hair. In this case, it is "red-orange".

Back in the days of "Color Fillers", we first put in the yellow (gold) filler and then put in the red filler in order to make orange. This is why it was called "The Building Blocks of Color".

However, today, all you have to do is to select a demi-color shade that is "light orange," or something in the orange category, to give you the base you need. (Tahitian Red Blonde works great).

Steps to a Tint Back

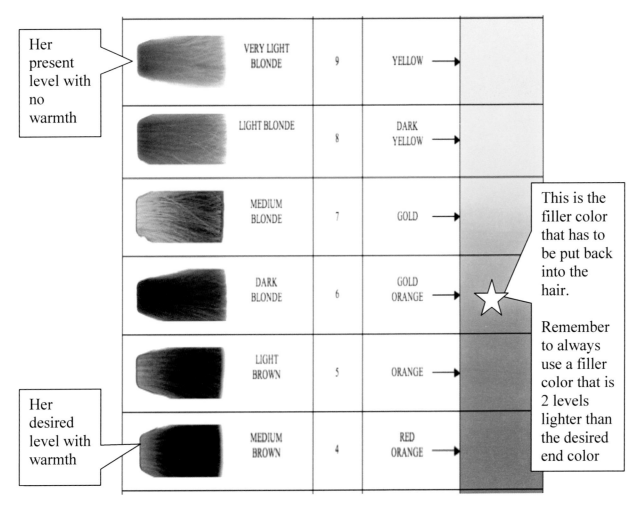

Her present level with no warmth → VERY LIGHT BLONDE — 9 — YELLOW →

This is the filler color that has to be put back into the hair.

Remember to always use a filler color that is 2 levels lighter than the desired end color

Her desired level with warmth → MEDIUM BROWN

Level	Tone
VERY LIGHT BLONDE (9)	YELLOW
LIGHT BLONDE (8)	DARK YELLOW
MEDIUM BLONDE (7)	GOLD
DARK BLONDE (6)	GOLD ORANGE
LIGHT BROWN (5)	ORANGE
MEDIUM BROWN (4)	RED ORANGE

WARNING:

It is very important to use a shade that is at least two levels lighter than your final desired color so that the end result won't look orange.

Apply the light orange demi-color (mixed with the appropriate developer) to the entire head and allow to process for about 15 to 20 minutes. Then use a clean towel and wipe off the demi-color or rinse the demi-color out at the shampoo bowl (do not shampoo, just rinse with water).

Next, mix and apply your final desired shade.

I would suggest that, for your final desired shade, you continue to use a demi-color. Since you are going darker and not needing any lifting action, a demi-color will hold better and keep the hair in better condition.

Also, for your final desired shade, stay away from ash shades. These may still result in drab and muddy looking hair. Instead, stick with the warmer gold or red shades for the best results. If you really want an ash finished look, use a natural / neutral base tint.

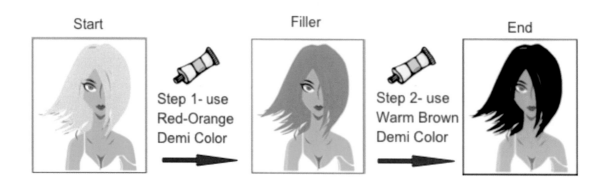

34

Color Corrective Procedures for

Brunettes

1. Dark Brown Tint Went Black

SITUATION:

After tinting your client's hair a dark brown shade, you realize that it went much darker than you expected. Maybe it even went black.

Warning: When this or any other hair color problem happens to you, do not let the client go home. You must make time immediately to fix the color before she leaves the salon. Not only should you do this to protect your reputation as a colorist, but also it is much easier to remove this dark hair color as soon as it has been done, as opposed to waiting even a few days.

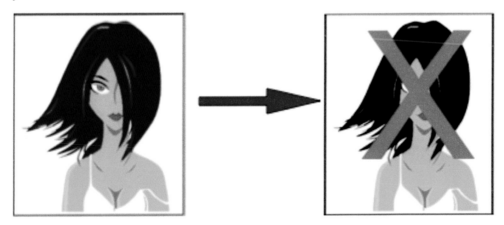

WHAT HAPPENED?

One of two things may have happened.

1) The dark brown shade you selected may have been too dark to begin with. This will usually happen when the hair is on the fine side. Remember that fine texture hair will always react faster and more extreme than a medium or coarse texture hair.

Haircolor Secret

Fine hair will go darker faster and deeper. Also, it will lighten faster and get lighter than other textures. In addition, it will react quicker to any chemical process such as perms and relaxers.

---

2) The client's hair is overly porous; therefore, the color was absorbed faster and darker than you expected. If you could see overly porous hair under a microscope, you would see that the hair has had the cuticle layer destroyed (torn off in patches exposing the cortex of the hair). Under a microscope, this looks a little like Swiss cheese because of the holes in the hair. What happens is that these holes actually become overly saturated with dye molecules and we perceive it as overly dark hair.

WHAT TO DO:

REMOVE THE DARK COLOR.

Once the hair is too dark, for whatever reason, the first thing you must do is remove some of the dark color with a lightener type product.

At the shampoo bowl, dampen the hair with water first, and then apply a mild bleach lightener (10 Vol.) mixture right at the shampoo bowl.

At this point, the ammonia vapors from the lightener will be very strong and rise up into your face. Therefore, have an assistant stand there fanning you and your client so you can both breathe. (I find a *Bazaar* magazine to work perfect for the fan).

Begin applying the lightener to the mid-shaft and then to the ends.

Work in the product with both hands (by dampening the hair first with a little water, you will get the lightener mixture through the hair more evenly and avoid having dry spots).

Wait a few minutes and, as soon as you see the color starting to lighten, apply the lightener to the re-growth area.

Watch the color closely. Remember, you don't want to lighten the hair too much. All you want to do is take off the very dark edge.

As soon as the darkest color starts to lighten, shampoo and condition the hair. Dry it completely to see the exact color.

If you are lucky, at this point, it may be the exact shade that you desire. If it is the shade you desire, you are finished.

But, more than likely, it will be some undesirable shade of reddish brown. This reddish brown shade is okay to have at this point (at least it's not black). This reddish brown shade is exactly what you need at this point as the base for your new brown shade.

RECOLORING:

There are a few things to keep in mind. The hair is very porous and it will go too dark again very easily, if you are not careful. You do not need the strength or the lift of a permanent color, so you should use a demi-color to recolor. You must do one or more test strands to see what your end result will be BEFORE you put the color all over the head.

Mix a small amount of two different shades of your demi-color, (maybe one from the ash series and one from the natural series). In the back of

the head, pull out 4 swatches of hair for your test strands. Apply each shade to 2 swatches. Set 2 timers, 1 for 5 minutes & 1 for 10 minutes.

After 5 minutes, clean off one of each color and do the same after the 10 minute timer goes off.

Now look at all 4 swatches, decide which one looks the best and go with it.

Note: If at 10 minutes the hair is still not dark enough, reapply your test strands and repeat the process.

HOW TO PREVENT THIS IN THE FUTURE:

During your initial color consultation, assess the hair's texture and porosity, and, if you feel the hair is on the fine side or the hair is dry and porous, go a little lighter with your color formulation and do one or more test strands.

Remember that if your finished color is too light, it's much easier to go back over it with a darker color if necessary as oppose to having to remove the color because it went too dark.

Haircolor Secret

Think light and always be right.

2 Brown Shade Looks Reddish

SITUATION:

After a brown tint has been completed, the client says her hair looks red.

WHAT HAPPENED?

Always keep in mind that any time you use an oxidative tint, you will create some warmth in the hair. This is especially true if you are trying to give your client a lighter shade of brown than her natural color (you are lifting and creating a lighter, redder color).

Many times, a client will ask you for something that is impossible to achieve and this is one. The request usually goes something like this.

"I think my hair just looks too dark and drab and I would like you to give me a lighter shade of brown, but I don't want to see any red. I just want a light caramel color."

At this point, you should let your client know that what she is asking for is impossible to do with a single process color. I am sure that someone will read this and wonder why I don't just recommend using an ash base color. But, if you read my comments about ash colors not really working the way we wish they would, in the book *Trade Secrets of How Haircolor Really Works* in this course, you will know that I never depend on ash colors or cool drabbers to do this job for me.

WHAT TO DO:

At this point, you need to recolor the hair with a demi-color, which is a little darker than the previous color.

WARNING: Be careful that the hair does not go too dark when you re-color it.

The reason that I suggest using a demi-color is because, since you have already colored her hair once, there should not be any Gray (non-pigmented) hair and the demi-color will tone down the red without getting any more lift.

After applying your demi-color, check in 5 minute and 10 minute intervals. Remove the demi-color, when your desired shade has been achieved.

HOW TO PREVENT THIS IN THE FUTURE:

Now that you know that it is impossible to make a "light brunette without any red", the next time you are faced with this situation do the following:

1) Use a demi-color instead of a permanent color.

Haircolor Secret

(Less Lift = Less Warmth)

---

2) Use an ash base color to help subdue the unwanted warm tone. But don't rely on it, because they never work as well as we wish they would.

3) If the red is still persistent, add a little blue mixtone "drabber" into your formula. Be careful, this could make the color look very dark.

4) Start taking your client's formula a little darker at each salon visit until the red is no longer apparent. Do this by using ¼ portion of the next darker color at each salon visit.

5) Don't try to give your client a brown color that is more than 2 levels lighter than her natural level.

3. Brown Tint Went too Dark on the Ends Only

SITUATION:

After you have completed the color service on a brunette, the re-growth area and mid-shaft look great but ,for some reason, the ends of the hair took way too dark.

WHAT HAPPENED?

This will usually occur on longer hair, which has overly porous ends due to blow-drying, tinting, brushing and environmental damage. The color was brought out to the ends and was left on too long. The overly porous ends of the hair absorbed too much tint too fast and the ends came out darker than the rest of the hair.

WHAT TO DO:

Mix a mild lightener solution of 10 volume. Take your client to the shampoo bowl and dampen her hair.

With your client sitting at the shampoo bowl and with her hair back in the sink, apply the lightener solution with your gloved hands to the dark areas only. Try not to get the lightener any higher up than necessary.

Work the lightener solution gently into the hair with your hands and watch the color closely. As soon as you see the very darkest parts starting to lighten, shampoo out the lightener.

This lightening action could take anywhere from just a few seconds to several minutes. Be sure to stand there and watch it closely, do not apply the lightener and leave the client unattended.

Exotic Brunettes

In most cases, this will be all you will have to do. However, if you leave the lightener on too long, the hair will look reddish, which means that you'll now have to go back over it and re-tint the ends.

To do this, I recommend using a demi-color. Reapply it to the red area only and watch it very carefully. Remove when the desired shade has been achieved.

HOW TO PREVENT THIS IN THE FUTURE:

If the ends of the hair look dry or porous, be very careful applying color to them. If the ends of the hair look good (not faded) when your client comes in for a touchup, don't even bring the color out over the ends at all. For some unknown reason, we seem to think that every time a client comes in for a touchup, we have to always bring the color out over her ends even if the ends don't need it.

If the ends are in need of color, but you think that they may grab too dark, first apply your touchup to the re-growth area. Then, while the color is processing, pull out 2 test strands in the back of the head. Bring out your color to each test strand and set 2 timers, one for 5 minutes and one for 10 minutes. Continue working with the test strands in this fashion until the exact timing is determined.

4 Brown Tint Took too Dark in the Temples

SITUATION:

After you have completed the tinting service, you realize that the color looks great everywhere except that the temples look way too dark.

WHAT HAPPENED?

The reason that the temples took so dark is because the hair in that area of the head could be very fine and fine hair will always take faster and deeper when dark haircolor is applied.

WHAT TO DO:

The dark color must be removed. Mix a bleach lightener with 20 volume. With a tint brush, apply the lightener mixture to the dark area only. Leave on just for a few moments until you see the color start to lighten, then shampoo out the lightener.

HOW TO PREVENT THIS IN THE FUTURE:

Exotic Brunettes

When you have a client to whom you know this happens, make sure that you write it down on the client record card.

The next time the client comes in, apply the touchup to the rest of the head and leave out the hairline. Wait for about 15 minutes, and then apply the color to the hairline. Also, if this problem continues, try mixing a small amount of a slightly lighter formula just to be used at the temples.

5. Brown Tint Looks Reddish in the Re-growth Area Only

SITUATION:

After a color application, the brown tint looks great at the mid-shaft and ends but the re-growth area (roots) look reddish.

WHAT HAPPENED?

This typically happens when a permanent color was used that was a little too light and some lift occurred at the re-growth area. The re-growth area (also called "the roots") is very delicate to any chemical process. This is due to two main reasons:

1) It is so close to the head that the color actually will process differently than the rest of the hair due to the body heat coming up from the scalp,

2) The hair is so new that the keratin (a protein that the hair is made from) hasn't had a chance to harden yet (keratinize). It is still in a very soft state and very susceptible to all chemical processes.

WHAT TO DO:

Simply mix a demi-color to match the rest of the hair and reapply it to the re-growth only. Check frequently after about 10 minutes and remove when the desired shade has been produced. This will usually take within 10 -20 minutes.

HOW TO PREVENT THIS IN THE FUTURE:

If this is happening because you are using a permanent color, switch your client to a demi-color. If you are already using a demi-color, start gradually going a little darker with your re-growth formula.

Haircolor Secret

If you start making your re-growth formula darker, you may not want to use this same "new darker color" on the rest of the hair. In this case, you would need to start using two different formulas (one for the new re-growth and one for the rest of the hair) at each color service.

---

6. Brown Shade Becomes Red After Just A Few Weeks

SITUATION:

A client that you tinted into a lovely rich brunette shade calls in 2 - 3 weeks to tell you her brown hair has turned red.

WHAT HAPPENED?

More than likely, the brown shade that you used was a permanent color. Remember that a permanent color must lift the natural color some and open the cuticle layer of the hair before it can deposit the artificial color pigment.

On the day of the service, the color has the full intensity of the artificial dye and will look dark, rich and beautiful. However, after a few weeks of shampooing and blow-drying, the darkest part of the color (blue pigments) will begin to fade. Since the natural color has been lifted during the oxidative process, you will now see the hair's "exposed contributing color pigment", which is reddish brown.

WHAT TO DO:

To correct this red color, you need to retint it with a deposit only color such as a demi-color. These demi-colors work great in these types of color correction procedures because of the following:

1. They will simply deposit your desired shade without getting any more lifting.

2. Demi-colors have a high degree of conditioning agents and glossers built into them, so they will leave the hair very shiny and healthy looking.

3. Demi-colors will fade as well but, because they cause very little or no lifting action, they will not expose a client's contributing color pigment. With prolonged use, they will not go red. (Unless you use a red shade, of course).

4. When a demi-color fades, it does what I call *"fades on tone"*. This means that, instead of the color going from brown to red, the color will go from brown to a lighter shade of brown. It literally "fades on tone". This happens because this type of color does not lift, and, therefore, it does not expose the client's contributing color pigment like a permanent color would.

HOW TO PREVENT THIS IN THE FUTURE:

The best way to minimize or eliminate this problem is to switch your client from permanent color and simply use demi-color in the future. This will expose the absolute minimum amount of your client's contributing color pigment and, therefore, give her the longest lasting brown color possible.

If you feel the need to use a permanent color because a demi-color does not give adequate gray coverage, read my "Top Ten List for Using Demi-Color" in the book *Trade Secrets of How Haircolor Really Works* in this course. There you will find several techniques on how to tweak demi-colors so they will perform better for you.

To continue your haircolor education, learn advanced levels of haircolor formulation and how to correct any possible haircolor situation, see the other books in the

Trade Secrets of a Haircolor Expert Course

Other Haircolor Education Programs
From David Velasco

HaircolorTradeSecrets.com

FREE Haircolor Ebook
Haircolor Books - Creative Foiling DVD's - Audio CD's

Trade Secrets of a Haircolor Expert
     David Velasco

HaircolorClubhouse.com

FREE Haircolor VIDEOS
Network with Thousands of Hairdressers - Haircolor BLOGS - Haircolor Photos

 The Haircolor Experts
"Networking Club House"
by David Velasco

HaircolorUniversity.com

12 Month - MultiMedia E-Course in the Art of Haircolor
Streaming and Downloadable - Videos - Audios - PDF

Haircolor University
By David Velasco

David Velasco "LIVE" Class DVD's

Available at:
HaircolorTradeSecrets.com

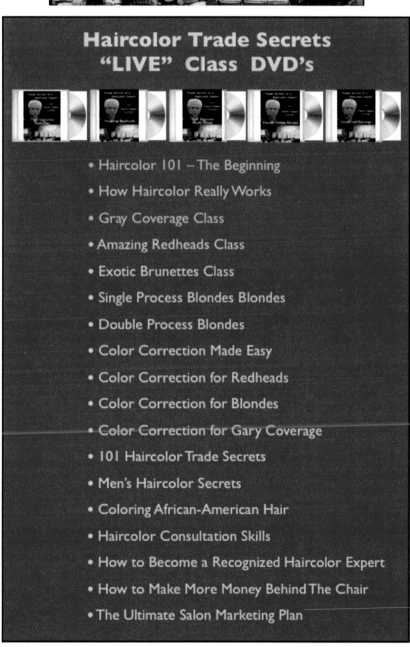

Haircolor Trade Secrets
"LIVE" Class DVD's

- Haircolor 101 – The Beginning
- How Haircolor Really Works
- Gray Coverage Class
- Amazing Redheads Class
- Exotic Brunettes Class
- Single Process Blondes Blondes
- Double Process Blondes
- Color Correction Made Easy
- Color Correction for Redheads
- Color Correction for Blondes
- Color Correction for Gary Coverage
- 101 Haircolor Trade Secrets
- Men's Haircolor Secrets
- Coloring African-American Hair
- Haircolor Consultation Skills
- How to Become a Recognized Haircolor Expert
- How to Make More Money Behind The Chair
- The Ultimate Salon Marketing Plan

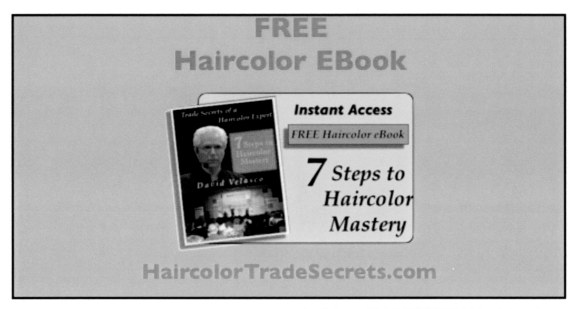

HAIRCOLOR TERMINOLOGY GLOSSARY

ACCELERATOR...(See ACTIVATOR)

ACCENT COLOR... A concentrated color product that can be added to permanent, semi- permanent or temporary haircolor to intensify or tone down the color. Another word for concentrate.

ACID.... An aqueous (water based) solution having a pH less than 7.0 on the pH scale.

ACTIVATOR... An additive used to quicken the action or progress of a chemical. Another word for booster, accelerator, protenator or catalyst.

ALKALINE.... An aqueous (water based) solution having a pH greater than 7.0 on the pH scale. The opposite of acid.

ALLERGY...... A physical reaction resulting from extreme sensitivity to exposure, contact and/or ingestion of certain foods or chemicals.

ALLERGY TEST... A test to determine the possibility or degree of sensitivity; also known as a patch test, predisposition test or skin test.

AMINO ACIDS.... The group of molecules that the body uses to synthesize protein. There are 22 different amino acids found in living protein that serve as units of structure.

AMMONIA.... A colorless pungent gas composed of hydrogen and nitrogen; in water solution is called ammonia water. Used in haircolor to swell the cuticle. When mixed with hydrogen peroxide, it activates the oxidation process on melanin, and allows the melanin to decolorize.

AMMONIUM HYDROXIDE..... An alkali solution of ammonia in water; commonly used in the manufacturing of permanent haircolor, lightener preparations and hair relaxers.

ANALYSIS (HAIR).... An examination of the hair to determine its condition and natural color. (SEE CONSULTATION, CONDITION)

AQUEOUS..... Descriptive term for water solution or any medium that is largely composed of water.

ASH... A tone or shade dominated by greens, blues, violets or grays. May be used to counteract unwanted warm tones.

BASE (ALKALI)... (See pH; ALKALINE)

BASE COLOR.... (See COLOR BASE)

BLEACH... (See LIGHTENER)

BLEEDING... Seepage of tint/lightener from the packet containing the hair to be colored or frosting cap due to improper application.

BLENDING.... A merging of one tint or tone with another.

BLONDING... A term applied to lightening the hair.

BONDS.... The means by which atoms are joined together to make molecules.

BOOSTER... (See ACTIVATOR)

BRASSY TONE... Undesirable red, orange or gold tones in the hair.

BREAKAGE... A condition in which hair splits and breaks off.

BUFFER ZONE... Applying color away from the scalp to avoid chemical overlapping.

BUILD-UP... Repeated coatings on the hair shaft.

BUMPING THE BASE... A term used to describe a gentle degree of lift of the natural color.

CATALYST... A substance used to alter the speed of a chemical reaction.

CATEGORY... A method of defining natural hair to help determine the undertones.

CAUSTIC... Strongly alkaline materials. At very high pH levels, can burn or destroy protein or tissue by chemical action.

CERTIFIED COLOR... A color which meets certain standards for purity and is certified by the FDA.

CERTIFIED HAIRCOLORIST.... A haircolorist who has passed a rigid examination process established by the American Board of Certified Haircolorists.

CETYL ALCOHOL... Fatty alcohol used as an emollient. It is also used as a stabilizer for emulsion systems, and in haircolor and cream developer as a thickener.

CHELATING STABILIZER.... A molecule that binds metal ions and renders them inactive.

CHEMICAL CHANGE... Alteration in the chemical composition of a substance.

CITRIC ACID.... Organic acid derived from citrus fruits and used for pH adjustment. Primarily used to adjust the acid-alkali balance. Has some antioxidant and preservative qualities. Used medicinally as a mild astringent.

COATING... Residue left on the outside of the hair shaft.

COLOR... Visual sensation caused by light.

COLOR ADDITIVE... (see ACCENT COLOR)

COLOR BASE... The combination of dyes which make up the tonal foundation of a specific haircolor.

COLOR LIFT... The amount of change natural or artificial pigment undergoes when lightened by a substance.

COLOR MIXING... Combining two or more shades together for a custom color.

COLOR REFRESHER... (1) Color applied to midshaft and ends to give a more uniform color appearance to the hair. (2) Color applied by a shampoo-in method to enhance the natural color. Also called color wash, color enhancer, color glaze.

COLOR REMOVER.... A product designed to remove artificial pigment from the hair.

COLOR TEST.... The process of removing product from a hair strand to monitor the progress of color development during tinting or lightening.

COLOR WHEEL.... The arrangement of primary, secondary and tertiary colors in the order of their relationships to each other. A tool for formulating.

COMPLEMENTARY COLORS... A primary and secondary color positioned opposite each other on the color wheel. When these two colors are combined, they create a neutral color. Combinations are as follows: Blue/Orange, Red/Green, Yellow/Violet.

CONCENTRATE... (See ACCENT COLOR)

CONDITION.... The existing state of the hair; its elasticity, strength, texture, porosity and evidence of previous treatments.

CONSULTATION.... Verbal communication with a client to determine desired result. [See ANALYSIS (HAIR)]

CONTRIBUTING PIGMENT... The current level and tone of the hair. Refers to both natural contributing pigment and decolorized (lightened) contributing pigment. (See UNDERTONE)

COOL TONES... (See ASH)

CORRECTIVE COLORING... The process of correcting an undesirable color.

CORTEX.... The second layer of hair. A fibrous protein core of the hair fiber, containing melanin pigment.

COVERAGE... Reference to the ability of a color product to color gray, white or other colors of hair.

CUTICLE.... The translucent, protein outer layer of the hair fiber.

CYSTEIC ACID.... A chemical substance in the hair fiber, produced by the interaction of hydrogen peroxide on the disulfide bond (cystine).

CYSTINE.... The disulfide amino acid, which joins protein chains together.

D & C COLORS.... Colors selected from a certified list approved by the Food and Drug Administration for use in drug and cosmetic products.

DECOLORIZE... A chemical process involving the lightening of the natural color pigment or artificial color from the hair.

DEGREE.... Term used to describe various units of measurement.

DEMI-COLOR... (See DEPOSIT-ONLY COLOR)

DENSE.... Thick, compact, or crowded.

DEPOSIT.... Describes the color product in terms of its ability to add

67

color pigment to the hair. Color added equals deposit.

DEPOSIT-ONLY COLOR... A category of color products between permanent and semi-permanent colors. Formulated to only deposit color, not lift. They contain oxidative dyes and utilize a low volume developer.

DEPTH... The lightness or darkness of a specific haircolor. (See VALUE, LEVEL)

DEVELOPER.... An oxidizing agent, usually hydrogen peroxide that reacts chemically with coloring material to develop color molecules and create a change in natural haircolor.

DEVELOPMENT TIME (OXIDATION PERIOD).... The time required for a permanent color or lightener to completely develop.

DIFFUSED.... Broken down, scattered; not limited to one spot.

DIRECT DYE.... A preformed color that dyes the fiber directly without the need for oxidation.

DISCOLORATION... The development of undesired shades through chemical reaction.

DOUBLE PROCESS... A technique requiring two separate procedures in which the hair is decolorized or prelightened with a lightener, before the depositing color is applied.

DRAB... Term used to describe haircolor shades containing no red or gold. (See ASH, DULL)

DRABBER.... Concentrated color used to reduce red or gold highlights.

DULL.... A word used to describe hair or haircolor without sheen.

DYE.... Artificial pigment.

DYE INTERMEDIATE... A material, which develops into color only after reaction with developer (hydrogen peroxide). Also known as oxidation dyes.

DYE REMOVER (SOLVENTS)... (See COLOR REMOVER)

DYE STOCK.... (See COLOR BASE)

ELASTICITY... The ability of the hair to stretch and return too normal.

ENZYME... A protein molecule found in living cells which initiates a chemical process.

EUMELANIN...A dark brown to almost black color pigment that determines the depth of the hairs natural color. (Eumelanin and

Pheomelanin are found in the cortex of the hair and are collectively known as Melanin)

FADE... To lose color through exposure to the elements or other factors.

FILLERS.... (1) Color product used as a color refresher or to replace undertones in damaged hair in preparation for haircoloring. (2) Any liquid-like substance to help fill the need for natural undertones. (See COLOR REFRESHER)

FORMULAS.... Mixture of two or more ingredients.

FORMULATE.... The art of mixing to create a blend or balance of two or more ingredients.

FROSTING... The introduction of lighter strands to the hair; generally executed with a frosting cap.

GLAZING... A term used to describe a translucent color used on the hair after a previous haircolor; a blending color.

GRAY HAIR. Hair with no natural pigment is actually white. White hairs look gray when mingled with pigmented hair.

HAIR..... A slender threadlike outgrowth on the skin of the head and body.

Exotic Brunettes

HAIR ROOT... That part of the hair contained within the follicle, below the surface of the scalp.

HAIR SHAFT.... Visible part of each strand of hair. It is made up of an outer layer called the cuticle, an innermost layer called medulla and an in-between layer called the cortex. The cortex layer is where color changes are made.

HARD WATER.... Water that contains minerals and metallic salts as impurities.

HENNA... A plant extracted coloring that produces bright shades of red. The active ingredient is lawsone. Henna permanently colors the hair by coating and penetrating the hair shaft. (See PROGRESSIVE DYE)

HIGH LIFT TINTING... A single process color with a higher degree of lightening action and a minimal amount of color deposit.

HIGHLIGHTING.... The introduction of a lighter color in small selected sections to increase lightness of the hair.

HYDROGEN PEROXIDE... An oxidizing chemical made up of 2 parts hydrogen, 2 parts oxygen (H_2O_2) used to aid the processing of permanent haircolor and lighteners. Also referred to as a developer; available in liquid or cream.

LEVEL... A unit of measurement used to evaluate the lightness or darkness of a color, excluding tone.

LEVEL SYSTEM... In haircoloring, a system colorists use to analyze the lightness or darkness of a haircolor.

LIFT.... The lightening action of a haircolor or lightening product on the hair's natural pigment.

LIGHTENER... The chemical compound which lightens the hair by dispersing, dissolving and decolorizing the natural hair pigment. (See PRE-LIGHTEN)

LIGHTENING.... (See DECOLORIZE)

LINE OF DEMARCATION... An obvious difference between two colors on the hair shaft.

LITMUS PAPER... A chemically treated paper used to test the acidity or alkalinity of products.

MEDULLA... The center structure of the hair shaft. Very little is known about its actual function.

MELANIN.... The tiny grains of pigment in the hair cortex which create natural haircolor.

MELANOCYTES... Cells in the hair bulb that manufacture melanin.

MELANOPROTEIN.... The protein coating of melanosome.

METALLIC DYES.... Soluble metal salts such as lead, silver and bismuth produce colors on the hair fiber, by progressive build-up and exposure to air.

MODIFIER.... A chemical found as an ingredient in permanent haircolors. Its function is to alter the dye intermediates.

MOLECULE... Two or more atoms chemically joined together; the smallest part of a compound.

NEUTRAL... (1) A color balanced between warm and cool, which does not reflect a highlight of any primary or secondary color. (2) Also refers to a pH of 7.

NEUTRALIZATION... The process that counter-balances or cancels the action of an agent or color.

NEUTRALIZE... Render neutral; counter-balance of action or influence. (See NEUTRAL)

NEW GROWTH... The part of the hair shaft that is between previously chemically treated hair and the scalp.

NONALKALINE.... (See ACID)

OFF THE SCALP LIGHTENER... Generally a stronger lightener (usually in powder form), not to be used directly on the scalp.

ON THE SCALP LIGHTENER... A liquid, cream or gel form of lightener that can be used directly on the scalp.

OPAQUE.... Allowing no light to shine through; flat; lack of translucency.

OUT GROWTH... (See NEW GROWTH)

OVER-LAP... Occurs when the application of color or lightener goes beyond the line of demarcation.

OVER POROUS... The condition where hair reaches an undesirable stage of porosity requiring correction.

OXIDATION.... (1) The reaction of dye intermediates with hydrogen peroxide found in haircoloring developers. (2) The interaction of hydrogen peroxide on the natural pigment.

OXIDATIVE HAIRCOLOR.... A product containing oxidation dyes which require hydrogen peroxide to develop the permanent color.

PARA TINT... A tint made from oxidation dyes.

PARA-PHENYLENEDIAMINE... An oxidative dye used in most permanent haircolors, often abbreviated as P.P.D.

PATCH TEST.... A test required by the Food and Drug Act. Performed by applying a small amount of the haircoloring preparation to the skin of the arm, or behind the ear to determine possible allergies (hypersensitivity). Also called pre- disposition or skin test.

PENETRATING COLOR.... Color that penetrates the cortex or second layer of the hair shaft.

PERMANENT COLOR.... (1) Haircolor products that do not wash out by shampooing. (2) A category of haircolor products mixed with developer that create a lasting color change.

PEROXIDE... (See HYDROGEN PEROXIDE)

PEROXIDE RESIDUE.... Traces of peroxide left in the hair after treatment with lightener or tint.

PERSULFATE.... In haircoloring, a chemical ingredient commonly used in activators that increases the speed of the decolorization process. (See

ACTIVATOR)

pH.... The quantity that expresses the acid/alkali balance. A pH of 7 is the neutral value for pure water. Any pH below 7 is acidic; any pH above 7 is alkaline. The skin is mildly acidic, and generally in the pH 4.5 to 5.5 range.

pH SCALE... A numerical scale from 0 (very acid) to 14 (very alkaline), used to describe the degree of acidity or alkalinity.

PHEOMELANIN...Red and Yellow pigments that give the hair warmth to the natural color. (Eumelanin and Pheomelanin are found in the cortex of the hair and are collectively known as Melanin)

PIGMENT.... Any substance or matter used as coloring; natural or artificial haircolor.

POROSITY.... Ability of the hair to absorb water or other liquids.

POWDER LIGHTENER... (See OFF THE SCALP LIGHTENER)

PREBLEACHING ... (See PRELIGHTEN)

PREDISPOSITION TEST.... (See PATCH TEST)

PRELIGHTEN.... Generally, the first step of double process haircoloring.

To lift or lighten the natural pigment. (See DECOLORIZE)

PRESOFTEN.... The process of treating gray or very resistant hair to allow for better penetration of color.

PRIMARY COLORS... Pigments or colors that are fundamental and cannot be made by mixing colors together. Red, yellow and blue are the primary colors.

PRISM.... A transparent glass or crystal that breaks up white light into its component colors -the spectrum.

PROCESSING TIME.... The time required for the chemical treatment to react on the hair.

PROGRESSIVE DYES OR PROGRESSIVE DYE SYSTEM... (1) A coloring system which produces increased absorption with each application. (2) Color products that deepen or increase absorption over a period of time during processing.

REGROWTH.... (See NEW GROWTH)

RESISTANT HAIR... Hair that is difficult to penetrate with moisture or chemical solutions.

RETOUCH.... Application of color or lightening mixture to new growth of hair.

SALT AND PEPPER... The descriptive term for a mixture of dark and gray or white hair.

SECONDARY COLOR... Colors made by combining two primary colors in equal proportion; green, orange and violet are secondary colors.

SEMI-PERMANENT HAIRCOLORING.... A pre-oxidized haircolor requiring no catalyst that lasts through several shampoos. It stains the cuticle layer, slowly fading with each shampoo.

SENSITIVITY... Skin that is highly reactive to the presence of a specific chemical. Skin reddens or becomes irritated shortly after application of the chemical. The reaction subsides when the chemical has been removed.

SHADE... (1) A term used to describe a specific color. (2) The visible difference between two colors.

SHEEN.... The ability of the hair to shine, gleam or reflect light.

SINGLE PROCESS COLOR... Refers to an oxidative tint solution that lifts or lightens, while also depositing color in one application. (See OXIDATIVE HAIRCOLOR)

78

SOFTENING AGENT... A mild alkaline product applied prior to the color treatment to increase porosity, swell the cuticle layer of the hair and increase color absorption. Tint that has not been mixed with developer is frequently used. (See PRE-SOFTEN)

SOLUTION... A blended mixture of solid, liquid or gaseous substances in a liquid medium.

SOLVENT... Carrier liquid in which other components may be dissolved.

SPECIALIST.... One who concentrates on only one part or branch of a subject or profession.

SPECTRUM.... The series of colored bands diffracted and arranged in the order of their wavelengths by the passage of white light through a prism. Shading continuously from red (produced by the longest wave visible) to violet (produced by the shortest):red, orange, yellow, green, blue, indigo and violet.

SPOT LIGHTENING... Color correcting using a lightening mixture to lighten darker areas.

STABILIZER... General name for ingredient, which prolongs life, appearance and performance of a product.

STAGE... A term used to describe a visible color change that natural haircolor goes through while being lightened.

STAIN REMOVER... Chemical used to remove tint stains from skin.

STRAND TEST... Test given before treatment to determine development time, color result and the ability of the hair to withstand the effects of chemicals.

STRIPPING... (See COLOR REMOVER)

SURFACTANT.... An abbreviation for Surface Active Agent. A molecule which is composed of an oil-loving (oleophillic) part and a water-loving (hydrophilic) part. They act as a bridge to allow oil and water to mix. Wetting agents, emulsifiers, cleansers, solubilizers, dispersing aids and thickeners are usually surfactants.

TABLESPOON.... 1/2 ounce; 2 teaspoons.

TEASPOON.... 1/6 ounce; 1/2 of a tablespoon.

TEMPORARY COLOR OR RINSES.... Color made from preformed dyes that are applied to the hair for short-term effect. This type of product is readily removed with shampoo.

TERMINOLOGY.... The special words or terms used in science, art or business.

TERTIARY COLORS.... The mixture of a primary and an adjacent secondary color on the color wheel. red-orange, yellow-orange, yellow-green, blue-green, blue-violet, red-violet. Also referred to as intermediary colors.

TEXTURE, HAIR.... The diameter of an individual hair strand. Termed: coarse, medium or fine.

TINT.... Permanent oxidizing haircolor product, having the ability to lift and deposit color in the same process. Requires a developer.

TINT BACK... To return hair back to its original or natural color.

TONE... A term used to describe the warmth or coolness in color.

TONER... A pastel color to be used after pre-lightening.

TONING. Adding color to modify the end result.
TOUCH-UP... (See RETOUCH)

TRANSLUCENT... The property of letting diffused light pass through.

TYROSINE.... The amino acid (tyrosine), which reacts together with the enzyme (tyrosinase) to form the hairs natural melanin.

TYROSINASE... The enzyme (tyrosinase) which reacts together with the amino acid (tyrosine) to form the hairs natural melanin.

UNDERTONE... The underlying color in melanin that emerges during the lifting process and contributes to the end result. When lightening hair, a residual warmth in tone always occurs.

UREA PEROXIDE... A peroxide compound occasionally used in haircolor. It releases oxygen when added to an alkaline color mixture.

VALUE.... (See LEVEL; DEPTH)

VEGETABLE COLOR.... A color derived from plant sources.

VIRGIN HAIR.... Natural hair that has not undergone any chemical or physical abuse.

VISCOSITY... A term referring to the thickness of a solution.

VOLUME.... The concentration of hydrogen peroxide in water solution. Expressed as volumes of oxygen liberated per volume of solution. 20 volume peroxide would thus liberate 20 pints of oxygen gas for each pint of solution.

WARM... A term used to describe haircolor. Containing red, orange, yellow or gold tones.

Collect the Full Series

and Create Your Own

Haircolor Education

Library

Volume 1 — English
Trade Secrets of a Haircolor Expert
Haircolor 101 The Beginning
David Velasco

Volume 2 — English
Trade Secrets of a Haircolor Expert
How Haircolor Really Works
David Velasco

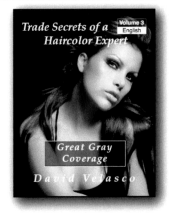

Volume 3 — English
Trade Secrets of a Haircolor Expert
Great Gray Coverage
David Velasco

Volume 4 — English
Trade Secrets of a Haircolor Expert
Amazing Redheads
David Velasco

Volume 5 — English
Trade Secrets of a Haircolor Expert
Exotic Brunettes
David Velasco

Volume 6 — English
Trade Secrets of a Haircolor Expert
Incredible Single Process Blondes
David Velasco

Volume 7 — English
Trade Secrets of a Haircolor Expert
Stunning Double Process Blondes
David Velasco

Volume 8 — English
Trade Secrets of a Haircolor Expert
Coloring African American Natural and Chemically Relaxed Hair
David Velasco & Pam Chambers

Volume 9 — English
Trade Secrets of a Haircolor Expert
Men's Haircolor
David Velasco

Volume 10 — English
Trade Secrets of a Haircolor Expert
101 Trade Secrets of a Haircolor Consultation

Exotic Brunettes

David Velasco

- *HAIRCOLOR SPECIALIST*
- *MASTER STYLIST*
- *SALON OWNER*
- *EDUCATOR*
- *CONSULTANT*
- *AUTHOR*

With 40 years Experience in the field of hairdressing, Velasco has become one of the industry's leading authorities.

Velasco began his career at the young age of 16 in Tampa.Fla. He soon moved to London, England where he worked and studied his craft with world-renowned hairdressers of that era.

Upon return to the USA Velasco began to develop his skills as an Educator and Effective Communicator while working with John & Suzzane Chadwick at the "Hair Fashion Development Center" on New York's 5th Ave.

By the age of 21 Velasco was STYLES DIRECTOR for the SAKS FIFTH AVE. beauty salon in New York City. Over the next 20 years Velasco became involved in almost every aspect of hair related activities possible. Including such achievements as, Freelance Hair Designer for photo sessions with major beauty publications and television commercials. He has held such prestige positions as Educational and Creative Consultant to CLAIROL INC., SHISEIDO LTD.,& THE WELLA CORP..

He has preformed as the Featured Guest Artist and Master Educator at hundreds of trade events throughout the world. His presentation at HAIRCOLOR U.S.A., symposium was rated BEST EDUCATIONAL EVENT by his peers.

Velasco has been a Contributing Author to many hair related articles for both consumer and professional publications and books. Velasco held a position as the NATIONAL ARTISTIC DIRECTOR FOR THE WELLA CORP. for ten years and is a member of the INTERNATIONAL HAIRCOLOR EXCHANGE.

Velasco was formally the DIRECTOR OF HAIRCOLOR for the world renowned BUMBLE & BUMBLE SALON in NEW YORK CITY and presently resides over his own salon David Velasco Salon, LTD. in Doylestown, Pennsylvania.

David and his Salon are proud members of INTERCOIFFURE MONDIAL, which is the most prestigious international hairdressing organization in the world.

As an industry leader, David is also owner of "Salon Success Systems Publications" through which he has Authored and Self-Published many books in the Art of Haircolor branded: **"Trade Secrets of a Haircolor Expert",** and produced a Series of Educational DVD's and a social networking website:**"The Haircolor Clubhouse"** where he provides free haircolor education to professional hairdressers around the world.

Made in the USA
Middletown, DE
20 June 2019